YOUR KNOWLEDGE HAS VALUE

- We will publish your bachelor's and
  master's thesis, essays and papers

- Your own eBook and book -
  sold worldwide in all relevant shops

- Earn money with each sale

Upload your text at www.GRIN.com
and publish for free

Bibliographic information published by the German National Library:

The German National Library lists this publication in the National Bibliography; detailed bibliographic data are available on the Internet at http://dnb.dnb.de .

Imprint:

Copyright © 2011 GRIN Verlag
Print and binding: Books on Demand GmbH, Norderstedt Germany
ISBN: 9783668937970

This book at GRIN:

https://www.grin.com/document/465452

Maximilian Mayr

Facebook and the influence on our daily lives

GRIN Verlag

GRIN - Your knowledge has value

Since its foundation in 1998, GRIN has specialized in publishing academic texts by students, college teachers and other academics as e-book and printed book. The website www.grin.com is an ideal platform for presenting term papers, final papers, scientific essays, dissertations and specialist books.

Visit us on the internet:

http://www.grin.com/

http://www.facebook.com/grincom

http://www.twitter.com/grin_com

Facharbeit

Facebook and the influence on our daily lives

Maximilian Mayr

Gymnasium auf der Karthause: E2/ 2011

Closing Date: 05/23/11

Table of Contents

1. Introduction

I have chosen this topic because I am very interested in social media in general. I use Facebook very often and it is astonishing that almost everybody of my friends is registered on Facebook as well. In my opinion the new way to communicate with people via the Internet and especially via Facebook is a revolution, just like the invention of the cell phone. Furthermore I am interested in figuring out the possibilities and chances that Facebook brings along. Although there are very much benefits Facebook offers, sometimes I have heard about criticism as well. I am looking forward to finding out detailed information about Facebook to be able to use the social networking service as efficient as possible in the near future.

2. An overview of Facebook

Facebook is with over 500 million users the world's largest social network. The Ex-Harvard student Mark Zuckerberg founded it in February 2004 and originally only Harvard students were allowed to join the network.[1] After just a week Facebook had nearly 3000 users, and Mark got E- Mails from other college students requesting to join his network.[2]

Since September 2006 everyone is able to join this network. You have to be at least 13 years old and you have to sign up at www.facebook.com with your real name and an existing E- Mail address.[3]

In January 2011 Goldman Sachs invested about $500 million in Facebook. This deal values the company at $50 billion. After this investment Facebook announced that they would begin to report their financial results by April 2012 because Facebook is going to be a possible candidate for an Initial Public Offer.[4]

With the help of Facebook, users are able to create and customize their own online profile very easily. They are capable of indicating their hobbies or just write some general information about themselves. Moreover they are able to connect to other real friends when they send a friend request to them.

All users have a wall, which is almost the same like a guestbook. But they can do much more with this wall as they can do with a normal guestbook. For example they are able to share

[1] cf. http://www.crunchbase.com/company/facebook (Updated: 03/29/11)

[2] cf. The Facebook Effect, David Kirkpatrick, 2010: S. 35

[3] cf. http://www.techterms.com/definition/facebook (Published: 01/14/08)

[4] cf. http://topics.nytimes.com/top/news/business/companies/facebook_inc/index.html (Updated: 03/29/11)

websites, photos or videos, so everyone who is connected to you can see what you have posted on your personal wall and comment on it.

Another basic function of Facebook is the personal message which is similar to a normal E- Mail. It is useful to use this function when you want to talk to someone in private. As a user you are also able to set many different privacy settings. For example you can restrict people from watching your profile in case they aren't connected to you.

Facebook can be used for many different things. For example you can use Facebook to stay in touch with friends you don't see very often, you can find new friends, you can play online games, you can share every kind of multimedia application, or you can just look for what your friends are doing at the moment.[5]

3. Reasons why Mark Zuckerberg founded Facebook

Mark Zuckerberg is the founder and the Chief Executive Officer of Facebook. He is born in Dobbs Ferry on the 14th of May 1986. He has studied Computer Science at Harvard University.[6] His father Edward Zuckerberg is a dentist and his mother Karen is a psychiatrist. He has three sisters, and when he got his first computer he was about 12 years old. He immediately developed a large interest for working with a computer and for creating useful programs like the "Zucknet", a program that allowed the Zuckerberg family to communicate within the house via electronic devices.[7]

After the release of the film "The Social Network", which deals with Mark Zuckerberg's college life and the story of founding Facebook, Mark gave several interviews in which he clearly says that the film doesn't show the real story behind Facebook. Many important facts are wrong depicted. For example when you watch the film, you get the impression that Zuckerberg founded Facebook because he wanted to impress some girls from his university or because he searched for social contacts. But in truth he had a completely different intention to found Facebook.[8] He aimed to make the world a more open place and he wanted to enhance the relationships of people who already know each other, so that they can understand the world around them better. He never wanted to get rich with his projects; he only wanted people to get out more of their lives. Even as the company was huge and very successful,

[5] cf. http://www.facebook.com (Updated: 04/12/11)
[6] cf. http://www.facebook.com/zuck (Updated: 04/26/11)
[7] cf. http://www.biography.com/articles/Mark-Zuckerberg-507402 (Updated: 04/26/11)
[8] cf. http://gawker.com/#!5666923/facebook-founder-says-his-intentions-were-pure (Updated: 08/18/10)

Zuckerberg wasn't interested in maximizing the profit by selling advertising; he wanted to increase the efficiency of his platform to keep the users happy.[9]

Marc Zuckerberg said: *"We're a utility. We're trying to increase the efficiency through which people can understand their world. We're not trying to maximize the time spent on our site. We're trying to help people have a good experience and get the maximum amount out of that time".*[10]

4. Reasons for the great success of Facebook based on differences to other social networks

Although Facebook is called a social network just as MySpace or Twitter, it is the most used and popular one. One reason for being the most successful social network deals with the term privacy. In contrast to MySpace, Facebook allows its users to limit particular pieces of information for certain target groups. MySpace also has different privacy settings, but compared with Facebook users of MySpace aren't able to customize their privacy settings in an appropriate way. Either you have a public profile, or you have a very exclusive profile. But on Facebook you are able to have both at the same time. On the one hand you can hide very secret information, and on the other hand you're able to publish information that is not very private.[11]

Furthermore the Facebook page is constructed more straightforward than the MySpace page. As a user who isn't that schooled and experienced in dealing with computers and especially with the Internet, joining and interacting on Facebook is much more easier than it is on MySpace. Facebook is very self- explanatory, so after using it for a short while you know almost everything what you need to know to use it correctly.[12]

But the most important difference to other social networks is the News Feed function of Facebook. This function shows the latest news on the users page based on how many of his or her friends have interacted with the specific piece content. For example when two of your friends share two different contents and content A is not as often commented, watched or liked as content B, you will see content B at the top of your News Feed list. With the help of

---

[9] cf. The Facebook Effect, David Kirkpatrick, 2010: S. 11/43
   cf. http://www.youtube.com/watch?v=v32AABzvCyc (Updated: 04/26/11)
[10] The Facebook Effect, David Kirkpatrick, 2010: S. 10
[11] cf. http://news.cnet.com/8301-13515_3-9730290-26.html (Published: 15.06.07)
[12] cf. http://www.facebook.com (Updated: 04/28/11) / cf. http://www.myspace.com (Updated: 04/28/11)

this function users will never get bored, they always will be informed about the latest news in their network.[13]

5. Dangers of Facebook

5.1 Loss of privacy

The biggest danger for users of Facebook is the loss of privacy. Most users of Facebook don't think about who is able to see their online activities. Although Facebook offers its users many possibilities to customize their privacy settings, only the fewest use them correctly. For example they are able to restrict certain target groups (for example people they aren't connected to) to search for them and to send them a friend request or a personal message. Furthermore the users of Facebook can determine which parts of their profile they want to show in public and which they want to keep secret. For example they can allow selected target groups to see which school they visit or which job they have, but at the same time they can restrict them to see where they live or to have a look at the activities on their personal wall. The problem is that Facebook doesn't challenge new users to optimize their privacy settings before taking part in the social network. Users often post photos without thinking of who will see them.[14] And especially youth people who apply for jobs and for universities should pay attention which information they publish on their online profiles. Many users don't know that not only their friends watch their online activities.

"A 2009 poll of U.S. employers found that 35 percent of companies had rejected applicants because of information they found on social networks."[15]

Even the president Barack Obama himself said in front of a group of high school students: *"I want everybody here to be careful about what you post on Facebook, because in the YouTube age, whatever you do will be pulled up later somewhere in your life."* He delivered this speech because there was an incident with Jon Favreau the speechwriter of Obama. A friend published a photo on Facebook that shows Favreau on the breast of a cardboard of Hillary Clinton.[16]

---

[13] cf. http://kenyarmosh.com/blog/7-reasons-why-facebook-is-rocking/ (Published: 05/22/07)
[14] cf. http://www.facebook.com (Updated: 04/28/11)
[15] The Facebook Effect, David Kirkpatrick, 2010: S. 204/205
[16] The Facebook Effect, David Kirkpatrick, 2010: S. 204/205

5.2 Cyber crime

Another big danger for Facebook users is cyber-crime. Unfortunately none of your personal data is really safe on Facebook, but there is no difference to other Internet platforms. There are, and there always will be hackers who are capable of hacking the passwords of online accounts to get access to private information.

Due to being the world's largest social network, Facebook is full of applications, games and advertising that contains spyware, malware or other harmful programs, which try to control your profile or to get secret information of you.[17] In fact the very famous game FarmVille with over 47 million active users monthly[18], violated the privacy settings of Facebook. Personal information including the "Facebook ID" (a unique identity number that every user of Facebook has since he is registered) of FarmVille users and even friends of FarmVille users was transmitted to different advertising and data companies. The problem is that with the help of the Facebook ID anyone is able to have a closer look at your online Facebook profile regardless whether the user has the most strict privacy settings or not. RapLeaf is one of the companies who obtained personal data from Facebook applications. RapLeaf used these Facebook IDs for their own database to sell private information from Facebook users. Shortly afterwards Facebook has limited the permission from RapLeafs to interact on Facebook.[19]

5.3 The effects of being dependent on Facebook

The average Facebook user log on to Facebook every day, has 130 friends, creates 90 pieces of content each month, and is connected to about 90 groups, pages or events.[20] This statistic shows some kind of dependence that is not to underestimate. Facebook has developed to a platform that is able to create psychological dependency. There are people who share almost everything of their lives, no matter how private, familiar or intimate the information is. It is frightening that everybody who is connected to somebody, no matter how close his or her relationship is in real life, is able to see what somebody post or share on his or her wall. At the

---

[17] cf. http://www.facebook.com (Updated: 04/28/11)

[18] cf. http://www.facebook.com/FarmVille (Updated: 04/28/11)

[19] cf. http://online.wsj.com/article/SB10001424052702304772804575558484075236968.html
(Published: 08/18/10) / cf. http://kotaku.com/#!5667215/report-farmville-breaks-facebook-privacy-rules-sends-personal-info-to-ad-firms (Published: 08/18/10)

[20] cf. http://www.facebook.com/press/info.php?statistics (Updated: 04/29/11)

present day Facebook users let their friends know when they wake up, what they are going to do, where they are at the moment and finally when they go to bed.[21]

Using Facebook has become some kind of competition for some people. There are many people who aspire after having as many friends as possible to impress their friends and to show them how popular they are. The problem is that they add some people they don't know, just to increase their amount of friends in Facebook.[22]

On the one hand to be connected to strangers includes very big dangers because when you get connected to people you have never seen before, they are able to follow almost every activity you perform on Facebook, dependent on your personal privacy settings. And on the other hand, when somebody uses Facebook in that way, he misunderstood the function of social networks in general.[23] All users of Social Networks should know the idea behind a Social Network; otherwise he or she is going to destroy the concept of social networking.

As a result of being contingent on Facebook or other social networks, various dangers are going to emerge. One example is the loss of true social contacts. Even for people who haven't got many friends and who aren't self opinionated in their real life, social networks such as Facebook are a possibility to give them the feeling of being somebody. They search for appreciation and confirmation. But Facebook has not been created to help people in that way. These problems must be realised by the family or friends of such people. Otherwise they get more and more addicted to a virtual network and they probably will forget to live their real lives.[24]

---

[21] cf. http://www.facebook.com (Updated: 04/29/11)

[22] cf. http://www.facebook.com/pages/Trying-to-add-as-many-friends-as-possible/253834117564 (Updated: 04/29/11)

[23] cf. The Facebook Effect, David Kirkpatrick, 2010: S. 10/11/43

[24] cf. http://www.facebook.com (Updated: 04/29/11)

6. Benefits of Facebook

6.1 Benefits for commercial users

As a result of being the second most viewed website worldwide after Google[25], Facebook has developed to one of the most popular possibilities to make advertising. Advertisers are allowed to utilize personal information of a user such as the residence of a user, interests, hobbies or the age of a user or even pages to which a user is connected. With the help of this information the companies are able to customize and restrain the advertising to selected target groups.

The New York Times referred to a wedding photographer who is able to see the relationship status of people in his environment. And when he sees that somebody changed his status into "engaged", he is capable of making specialized advertising with a high success rate. The New York Times interviewed the wedding photographer and he said that he *"had good success with it on a limited budget"*.[26]

Consumer behaviour is another important advantage for commercial users of Facebook. Since 2007, Facebook sells advertising displaying selected profile pictures based on information of user activities that deals with consumer behaviour. With the help of status messages and content in terms of commercial messages, which is shared on Facebook, companies are able to evaluate the useful information to acquire consumer behaviour of Facebook users.[27]

6.2 Benefits for regular users

The huge amount of people using Facebook enables the chance to get connected to many people. For example you can communicate to relatives or to old friends you don't see very often. But communicating with your closest friends and your family via Facebook is very comfortable too; for example in case you are further afar from home.

Additionally you can find new friends with similar interests and hobbies. When you specify your online profile you are able to compare it to other online profiles, and when you find someone who has roughly the same interests and hobbies like you have, you can start thinking

---

[25] cf. http://mostpopularwebsites.net/ (Updated: 04/29/11)

[26] http://www.nytimes.com/2010/03/04/technology/04facebook.html?ref=business (Published: 03/03/10)

[27] cf. http://www.nytimes.com/2007/11/07/technology/07adco.html?scp=4&sq=marketing&st=Search (Published: 11/07/07)

about sending him or her a friend request to get connected and to start communicating with the person.[28]

Moreover the very common use of Facebook nowadays has developed the social network to a kind of discussion board for almost every topic, no matter whether it deals with politics, the latest news report or other general issues. Every Facebook user is allowed to join any kind of online discussion and to read comments of other users, so they are able to react on the comments immediately or simply utter their own opinion.[29]

7. Potential uses of Facebook by government agencies and politicians

7.1 The increasingly important role of Facebook in politics

Nowadays even government agencies and politicians have realized where people get their information from and which new possibilities the use of the Internet offers. Government agencies and politicians often use Facebook to promote themselves and the parties, which they are belonging to. They create their own public Facebook pages and groups, so that everybody is allowed to join and take part in actively. Just before important elections they present their party manifestos and advertise for themselves in different ways. For example they announce upcoming events or the latest news of their party. With these new concepts based on using modern media, they try to reach as much citizens as possible because they want to win new sympathisers for their party, and because they want to keep people informed who already support their party.

Further on government agencies try to reach and recruit new potential employees with the help of Facebook. Due to the new possibilities Facebook offers its users, potential sympathizers or potential employees get the impression of having direct contact to the law-givers, although they can't be sure whether they are really communicating with real politicians. In many cases the political parties have staffers who replace the politicians.[30] But the most important advantage, for politicians and even for all people who are political active, is that they can elude the press agencies with the help of Facebook. As a result of having direct contact to politically involved people, the government agencies are able to deliver

---

[28] cf. http://www.facebook.com (Updated: 04/29/11)

[29] cf. http://www.facebook.com/apps/application.php?id=2373072738&ref=ts#!/GuttenBack (Updated: 04/29/11)

[30] cf. http://abcnews.go.com/Politics/politicians-facebook-photos-videos-votes-reach-constituents/story?id=12358070 (Published: 12/15/10) / http://www.facebook.com/CDU (Updated: 05/16/11)

uncensored, transparent, genuine and unfiltered messages and opinions, which are not manipulated by the press corps.[31]

7.2 Further examples of how different government agencies make use of Facebook

The United States Environmental Protection Agency and even the USA.gov, the official web portal of the United States government, have created their own Facebook page where people are allowed to become a "fan". So they can be kept informed about the latest news or current events. Another possibility to take advantage of Facebook is to take part in the online discussions of those sites. Everybody can join and utter his or her opinion on those discussion boards.[32]

A further example is the NASA Goddard Space Flight Center. They use Facebook to communicate and to collaborate with universities or other colleagues who are working on similar projects. In this way they can improve the efficiency of their work.[33]

8. How Facebook has changed Egypt

8.1 The development of "The 6th of April Youth Movement"

Using Facebook in Egypt became common in 2008 when the Egyptian soccer team reached the final of the soccer league championship the first time. An Egyptian fan had the idea to create a Facebook group. Soon after the foundation, the group achieved about 45.000 members and many Egyptians started using Facebook. The second important event for Facebook being used frequently in Egypt deals with the riots in Mahalla al-Kubra. Worker of the textile industry originally wanted to start a protest on the 6th of April 2008, but protests are forbidden in Egypt. So Ahmed Maher, one of the founders of the 6th of April Youth

---

[31] cf. http://www.pbs.org/mediashift/2009/11/politicians-use-social-media-to-bypass-the-press-corps306.html (Published: 11/02/09)

[32] cf. http://www.facebook.com/eparegion10?ref=ts (Updated: 05/19/11)
    cf. http://www.facebook.com/USAgov (Updated: 05/19/11)

[33] cf. http://fcw.com/Articles/2009/04/20/Facebook-and-government-agencies.aspx (Published: 04/17/09)

Movement, started to publish and organize this protest via Facebook to initiate more demonstrations. [34]

The 6th of April Youth Movement is founded on March the 23rd. The aim of this group was to change the autocratic state Egypt into a more democratic state. Ahmed Maher began to send invitations to his Facebook friends, and at the end of March the Facebook group achieved about 40.000 members. After some violent demonstrations, induced by the 6th of April Youth Movement, the security forces of Egypt arrested Abdel-Fattah, the other founder of the 6th of April Youth Movement. But this imprisonment didn't stop her sympathizers to keep on protesting.

Ahmed Maher planned another demonstration for the 4th of May 2008, the 80th birthday of the president Mubarak. Afterwards he got arrested as well. After beating him about 12 hours, they released him. From now on it was very difficult for the security forces of Egypt to arrest him again. Meanwhile he was a very famous citizen and every time when they arrest him, the citizens would have triggered huge protests. [35]

8.2 The effects of the 6th of April Youth Movement on Egyptian politics

On the 25th of January 2011, further protests against the ex-president Hosni Mubarak started. The Egyptian citizens criticized Mubarak's politics in general and the consequential high unemployment and poverty rate of Egyptian. [36] Mubarak is known for his corrupt and autocratic governance since he became president of Egyptian in 1981 because he passed the Emergency Law to gain dictatorial authority. [37] The main organizer of these protests is the 6th of April Youth Movement.

This time the demonstrations had more supporter than ever before. For that reason the Egyptian government tried and succeeded in cutting off the Internet and Cell services on the 28th of January. [38] Fortunately the Egyptian found different ways to circumvent this barrier. [39]

These events were very important for local reporters. They started to use social media professionally to disseminate all kinds of current information. Thereafter Al Jazeera, an

---

[34] cf. http://www.zeit.de/politik/ausland/2011-02/jugendbewegung-aegypten-facebook?page=1 (Updated: 05/21/11)

[35] cf. http://www.zeit.de/politik/ausland/2011-02/jugendbewegung-aegypten-facebook?page=2 (Updated: 05/21/11)

[36] cf. http://www.huffingtonpost.com/2011/01/28/whats-going-on-in-egypt_n_815734.html (Updated: 03/30/11)

[37] cf. http://www.nytimes.com/2010/05/12/world/middleeast/12egypt.html (Published: 05/11/10)

[38] cf. http://mashable.com/2011/02/11/egyptian-president-steps-down/ (Published: 02/11/11)

[39] cf. http://www.nytimes.com/2011/01/29/technology/internet/29cutoff.html (Published: 01/28/11)

Arabic-language news network[40], was allowed to report for CNN. From now on the audience, who was informed about what happened in Egypt in detail, was even larger than before.[41] These circumstances determined Mubarak to finally resign on the 11th of February. In an army statement, the military announced to abolish the Emergency Law and to change the constitutions as soon as the protests end.[42]

9. Conclusion

After writing this "Facharbeit", I can proudly say that I am much more informed about Facebook and how it influences our daily lives. From now on I know very much about Mark Zuckerberg and the history of Facebook as a company. Mark Zuckerberg is a very interested and talented person with a good sense of modern trends. He has founded Facebook for the right reasons, and I think he is only that successful because he always was more interested in satisfying users than making money with his projects.

Facebook is the most successful social networking site, and although Facebook involves some dangers like cyber attacks or becoming addicted to Facebook, I fortunately can say that no one of them concerned me up to now. For the future I am well informed about how I can use Facebook safely and efficiently, so I have nothing to fear from.

Due to the great possibilities Facebook offers to government agencies, politicians and companies, it has developed to one of the most important and useful Internet platforms worldwide. Government agencies and politicians have a new platform to disseminate information and to advertise for themselves. Concerning these new possibilities, nowadays government agencies and politicians are able to confront more target groups with politics and important news than they could without this platform. Companies are enabled to make personalised advertising, so they are able to maximize their profits.

Furthermore Facebook and other social media proved their importance nowadays, when we look at what have happened in Egypt. The revolution in Egypt, initiated by groups of demonstrators who has communicated and organized their plans via Facebook, probably would never had occurred without the capabilities Facebook offers.

---

[40] cf. http://english.aljazeera.net/ (Updated: 05/21/11)

[41] cf. http://mashable.com/2011/02/11/egyptian-president-steps-down/ (Published: 02/11/11)

[42] cf. http://english.aljazeera.net/news/middleeast/2011/02/201121125158705862.html (Published: 02/11/11)

14

10. Bibliography

Literature:

- Kirkpatrick, David: The Facebook Effect: The Inside Story of the Company That Is Connecting the World, Simon & Schuster, New York 2010

Websites:

- cf. http://www.crunchbase.com/company/facebook (Updated: 3/29/11)

- cf. http://www.techterms.com/definition/facebook (Published: 01/14/08) / (Updated: 03/29/11)

- cf. http://topics.nytimes.com/top/news/business/companies/facebook_inc/index.html (Updated: 03/29/11)

- cf. http://www.facebook.com/zuck (Updated: 04/26/11)

- cf. http://www.biography.com/articles/Mark-Zuckerberg-507402 (Updated: 04/26/11)

- cf. http://gawker.com/#!5666923/facebook-founder-says-his-intentions-were-pure (Updated: 08/18/10)

- cf. http://www.youtube.com/watch?v=v32AABzvCyc (Updated: 04/26/11)

- cf. http://news.cnet.com/8301-13515_3-9730290-26.html (Published: 06/16/07) / (Updated: 04/26/11)

- cf. http://www.myspace.com (Updated: 04/28/11)

- cf. http://kenyarmosh.com/blog/7-reasons-why-facebook-is-rocking/ (Published: 05/22/07) / (Updated: 04/28/11)

- cf. http://www.facebook.com/FarmVille (Updated: 04/28/11)

- cf.http://online.wsj.com/article/SB10001424052702304772804575558484075236968. html (Published: 08/18/10) / (Updated: 04/29/11)

- cf. http://kotaku.com/#!5667215/report-farmville-breaks-facebook-privacy-rules-sends-personal-info-to-ad-firms (Published: 08/18/10) / (Updated: 03/29/11)

- cf. http://www.facebook.com/press/info.php?statistics (Updated: 04/29/11)

- cf. http://www.facebook.com/pages/Trying-to-add-as-many-friends-as-possible/253834117564 (Updated: 04/29/11)

- cf. http://mostpopularwebsites.net/ (Updated: 04/29/11)

- cf. http://www.nytimes.com/2010/03/04/technology/04facebook.html?ref=business (Published: 03/03/10) / (Updated: 04/29/11)

- cf.http://www.nytimes.com/2007/11/07/technology/07adco.html?scp=4&sq=marketin g&st=Search (Published: 11/07/07) / (Updated: 04/29/11)

- cf. http://www.facebook.com (Updated: 04/29/11)

- cf.http://www.facebook.com/apps/application.php?id=2373072738&ref=ts#!/GuttenB ack (Updated: 04/29/11)

- cf. http://abcnews.go.com/Politics/politicians-facebook-photos-videos-votes-reach-constituents/story?id=12358070 (Published: 12/15/10) / (Updated: 04/29/11)

- cf. http://www.facebook.com/CDU (Updated: 05/16/11)

- cf. http://www.pbs.org/mediashift/2009/11/politicians-use-social-media-to-bypass-the-press-corps306.html (Published: 11/02/09) / (Updated: 05/17/11)

- cf. http://www.facebook.com/eparegion10?ref=ts (Updated: 05/19/11)

- cf. http://www.facebook.com/USAgov (Updated: 05/19/11)

- cf. http://fcw.com/Articles/2009/04/20/Facebook-and-government-agencies.aspx (Published: 04/17/09) / (Updated: 03/29/11)

- cf. http://www.zeit.de/politik/ausland/2011-02/jugendbewegung-aegypten-facebook?page=1 (Updated: 05/21/11)

- cf. http://www.zeit.de/politik/ausland/2011-02/jugendbewegung-aegypten-facebook?page=2 (Updated: 05/21/11)

- cf. http://www.huffingtonpost.com/2011/01/28/whats-going-on-in-egypt_n_815734.html (Updated: 03/30/11)

- cf. http://www.nytimes.com/2010/05/12/world/middleeast/12egypt.html (Published: 05/11/10) / (Updated: 05/17/11)

- cf. http://mashable.com/2011/02/11/egyptian-president-steps-down/ (Published: 02/11/11) / (Updated: 05/17/11)

- cf. http://www.nytimes.com/2011/01/29/technology/internet/29cutoff.html (Published: 01/28/11) / (Updated: 05/17/11)

- cf. http://english.aljazeera.net/ (Updated: 05/21/11)

- cf. http://mashable.com/2011/02/11/egyptian-president-steps-down/ (Published: 02/11/11) / (Updated: 05/17/11)

- cf. http://english.aljazeera.net/news/middleeast/2011/02/201121125158705862.html
  (Published: 02/11/11) / (Updated: 05/17/11)